AI Money Machine

Unlock the Secrets to Making Money
Online with AI

Lucas Bennett

Contents

Chapter One

AI and Online Income Generation

Welcome to the exciting world where artificial intelligence (AI) meets online income generation. AI, a revolutionary force in the digital age, is reshaping the way we create, market, and monetize online.

By leveraging AI, entrepreneurs, freelancers, and digital marketers can tap into innovative methods to build their online presence, create compelling content, and find new avenues for revenue.

As we explore the possibilities that AI presents, you'll discover how it's not just about automating tasks, but about amplifying your creative potential and reaching new heights in online income generation.

Potential of AI for Diverse Audiences

AI's potential transcends various sectors, offering unique opportunities for a wide range of audiences. Entrepreneurs can harness AI for business analytics and market insights, optimizing their strategies for greater success. Tech enthusiasts can delve into AI's cutting-edge applications, staying ahead in the rapidly evolving technological landscape. Freelancers and digital marketers can leverage AI to enhance their services, from content creation to data-driven marketing campaigns. Career shifters looking for new opportunities can find AI a valuable tool to break into emerging fields. Lastly, those seeking passive income can utilize AI in automated trading, content generation, and more, making AI an indispensable asset in the pursuit of diverse income streams.

Practical Insights for Six-Figure Earnings

The upcoming chapters will delve into practical strategies for harnessing AI in various online income streams, each with the potential to reach or exceed six-figure annual earnings. From leveraging AI in affiliate marketing to using AI tools for efficient content creation and digital marketing strategies, the book will provide actionable insights for maximizing income in the AI-driven digital landscape.

Chapter Two

Affiliate Marketing

A ffiliate marketing has rapidly emerged as one of the most lucrative ways to generate income online. By promoting products or services and earning a commission for every sale or lead that is generated through their affiliate links, you can build a sustainable and profitable online business.

Basics of Affiliate Marketing

At its core, affiliate marketing involves three key players: the merchant (seller), the affiliate (marketer), and the customer. The merchant provides products or services, the affiliate promotes those products through various channels, and the customer makes a purchase or completes a desired action, such as filling out a form or signing up for a service. The affiliate receives a commission for driving the desired action.

Affiliate marketers typically leverage content marketing and persuasion techniques to attract and engage potential customers. Traditionally, creating high-quality content that appeals to the target audience has been a time-consuming process. However, with AI, the process of generating compelling content has become faster, more efficient, and scalable.

Selecting Niches and Products

Selecting the right niches and products is crucial in affiliate marketing. It's about connecting with the right audience and offering them what they actually want and need. Here's a straightforward approach to nail it:

First, dive into Amazon's Best Sellers. It's a goldmine for identifying trending products. It's like a cheat sheet showing what people are buying right now. You're not just guessing what's hot; you're seeing real-time data on what's flying off the virtual shelves. Whether it's tech gadgets, home goods, or fitness equipment, you're getting a direct line to what's popular.

Next, let's talk about Ahrefs. This tool is your secret weapon for niche keyword research. It's not just about finding any niche; it's about finding a profitable one with enough search volume without too much competition. Ahrefs helps you dig into what people are searching for related to these trending products. You're looking for those sweet-spot keywords that are like beacons to your target audience.

Using Amazon's Best Sellers for product trends and Ahrefs for keyword insights, you're setting yourself up for success. This combination is about being smart and strategic with your choices.

How to Use AI to Create Compelling Content

Utilizing AI tools like ChatGPT and Midjourney can significantly streamline your content creation process, especially in the context of affiliate marketing. These tools offer both efficiency and creativity in generating compelling content.

ChatGPT for Blog Posts

ChatGPT is invaluable for generating blog post ideas, outlines, and even full drafts. For instance, if you're promoting a line of skincare products, ChatGPT can help you create a detailed blog post on "5 Essential Skincare Routines for Different Skin Types." The AI can suggest key points to cover, provide relevant tips, and even draft sections of the content. This not only saves time but also ensures your content is informative, engaging, and SEO-friendly.

Canva for Social Media Graphics:

Canva is a powerhouse for creating stunning visuals. Whether you need eye-catching graphics for Instagram posts, Facebook banners, or Pinterest pins, Canva's user-friendly interface and extensive library of templates make it a go-to resource. For example, you can create a visually appealing Instagram post featuring the skincare products from your blog, highlighting their benefits or user testimonials. Canva's tools enable you to design graphics that align with your brand and appeal to your target audience, enhancing the attractiveness of your affiliate products.

Midjourney for Advanced Visuals:

Midjourney, another powerful AI tool, takes visual content creation to the next level. It's particularly useful for generating unique and high-quality images that stand out on social media. For example, you can use Midjourney to create a series of thematic images showcasing the lifestyle or the aspirational aspects of the skincare products you're promoting. These images could depict serene spa-like settings or happy customers, providing a more emotive and persuasive visual appeal.

Using ChatGPT, Canva, and Midjourney in tandem allows you to produce a cohesive and attractive content package for your affiliate marketing. ChatGPT helps with the ideation and creation of written content, while Canva and Midjourney ensure your visual content is both professional and engaging. This combination of AI tools empowers you to create content that not only draws the audience in but also keeps them engaged, ultimately driving success.

Strategies for Embedding Affiliate Links Effectively

Embedding affiliate links with AI assistance is a strategic move in affiliate marketing. AI can help you place these links in your content in a way that is both effective and unobtrusive. It's all about finding the right balance between promotion and maintaining the authenticity of your content.

AI for Strategic Link Placement:

AI tools can analyze your content and suggest optimal places to insert affiliate links. For instance, if you have a blog post about the latest tech gadgets, AI can identify key sections where readers might be most receptive to exploring the products, such as after a positive product feature or within a product comparison table. This ensures that the placement of affiliate links feels natural and contextually relevant, rather than forced or disruptive.

Maintaining a Balance:

While placing affiliate links is crucial, it's equally important to keep your content genuine and reader-focused. AI can help here too, by analyzing reader engagement and feedback. For example, AI can track which affiliate links get the most clicks and engagement, giving you insight into what your audience finds valuable. This data can guide you in creating future content that resonates with your audience while still promoting affiliate products effectively.

Authenticity is Key:

The goal is to provide value to your audience. Your content should always be informative, engaging, and truthful. AI can assist in maintaining this balance by suggesting ways to naturally integrate product mentions and links without making your content feel like a sales pitch.

This might mean weaving affiliate links into informative sections, tutorials, or personal experience stories related to the product.

By leveraging AI for strategic placement of affiliate links, you can enhance the effectiveness of your affiliate marketing efforts without compromising the integrity of your content. AI's analytical capabilities, combined with a focus on authenticity and providing value, create a powerful approach to embedding affiliate links. This method ensures that your content remains engaging and trustworthy while also serving your affiliate marketing goals.

Chapter Three

Faceless YouTube Channels

Creating faceless YouTube channels is an increasingly popular strategy in the digital content space, especially for those who prefer to remain anonymous or who want to focus solely on the content rather than personal branding. One of the key components of this strategy is scripting, and AI tools can play a significant role here.

Scripting with AI tools

AI tools like ChatGPT can be incredibly useful for scripting YouTube videos. These tools can help generate ideas, create outlines, and even write entire scripts based on the topic you're covering. For instance, if you're creating a channel focused on health and fitness, AI can help you script videos on topics like "10 Quick Home Workouts" or "Healthy Meal Prep for Beginners."

The AI can structure your script with an engaging intro, informative content body, and a compelling call-to-action. It can also ensure that your script has a natural flow, maintains viewer engagement, and is optimized for SEO, which is crucial for YouTube content.

Benefits of Scripting with AI:

- **Efficiency**: AI dramatically speeds up the scripting process, allowing you to produce content more quickly.

- **Consistency**: AI can help maintain a consistent tone and style across your videos, which is important for brand identity, even on a faceless channel.

- **SEO Optimization**: AI tools can suggest keywords and phrases to include in your script, improving your video's discoverability on YouTube.

- **Diversity in Content**: With AI assistance, you can easily explore a wide range of topics and formats, keeping your channel fresh and engaging.

Integrating AI-Scripted Content:

When using AI for scripting, it's important to personalize the content so that it doesn't sound robotic or generic. You should add your unique insights, experiences, or humor to make the content more relatable and engaging. AI scripts should serve as a foundation or starting point, which you can then build upon to create videos that resonate with your audience.

Creating faceless YouTube channels using AI-scripted content is a smart strategy for those looking to produce high-quality, engaging, and consistent content. By leveraging AI, you can focus on the creative aspects of content creation and streamline the more time-consuming aspects like scripting. This approach allows for a more efficient content creation process, enabling you to keep your channel active and appealing to your audience.

Techniques for video creation and editing

Creating captivating content is essential when you don't show your face on YouTube. Here are some techniques to enhance your video creation and editing process:

1. Choosing the Right Tools:
- **AI-Assisted Video Creation Tools:** Explore tools like Pictory, Lumen5, or InVideo. These platforms use AI to help create engaging videos from scripts, with various templates and stock footage.

- **Editing Software:** For more detailed editing, software like Adobe Premiere Pro or CapCut.

2. Scripting and Storyboarding:
- **AI Scripting:** Utilize AI tools like ChatGPT for scripting. Feed it the topic, and it generates a script that can be tweaked as needed.

- **Storyboarding:** Plan your video flow. While AI can't storyboard for you, use tools like Boords or Storyboard That for a visual layout of your video.

3. Voiceovers and Audio:

- **AI Voiceovers:** Tools like 11Labs or Descript offer AI-generated voiceovers that sound natural and engaging. Perfect for faceless channels where narration is needed.

- **Background Music:** Use royalty-free music libraries like Epidemic Sound, you can create your own using text prompts with Mubert or you can use YouTube's Audio Library.

4. Graphics and Visuals:

- **AI for Graphics:** Canva and other AI-based design tools can generate infographics, thumbnails, and other visual elements.

- **Animation Software:** For channels focusing on animated content, consider using Adobe After Effects or Vyond, which allow creation of animations without on-screen presence.

5. SEO Optimization:

- **Titles and Descriptions:** Use AI tools for keyword research to optimize your video titles, descriptions, and tags for better search visibility.

- **Thumbnail Creation:** Create compelling thumbnails using tools like Canva, ensuring they are eye-catching and relevant to the video content.

6. Consistency in Branding:

- **Brand Aesthetics:** Maintain a consistent color scheme, font style, and layout in your videos to establish brand identity.

- **Intro and Outro Clips:** Use standard intro and outro clips to give your videos a professional and consistent look.

7. Effective Editing Techniques:

- **Cutting and Trimming:** Learn basic editing skills to cut out unnecessary parts, keeping content engaging and to the point.

- **Transitions and Effects:** Use transitions sparingly and effects to enhance the storytelling without overwhelming the viewer.

8. Engagement Strategies:

- **Call to Actions:** Include calls to action in your videos, encouraging viewers to like, comment, subscribe, or follow a link.

- **Engaging Content:** Ensure the content is engaging and provides value, keeping viewers interested and reducing bounce rates.

9. Analytics and Improvement:

Feedback Incorporation: Actively seek and incorporate viewer feedback to continually improve video quality and relevance.

Monetizing YouTube channels

1. YouTube Partner Program (AdSense):

- **Eligibility and Setup:** Meet the YouTube Partner Program requirements, including having at least 1,000 subscribers and 4,000 watch hours over the past 12 months. Connect your channel to AdSense to start earning from ads displayed on your videos.

- **Ad Placement Strategies:** Optimize your content for advertiser-friendly content. Understand the types of ads (like skippable and non-skippable ads) and strategically place them in your videos for maximum revenue without compromising viewer experience.

2. Affiliate Marketing:

- **Affiliate Links in Descriptions:** Use your video descriptions to include affiliate links to products or services relevant to your content. Ensure transparency with your audience about these links.

- **Product Reviews and Recommendations:** Create content that naturally integrates product reviews or recommendations, aligning with your niche, and include your affiliate links.

3. Channel Memberships and Super Chats:

- **Memberships:** Offer channel memberships for exclusive content, badges, and perks to your subscribers for a monthly fee.

- **Super Chats and Super Stickers:** During live streams, enable Super Chats and Super Stickers to allow viewers to pay to highlight their messages.

4. Selling Merchandise:

- **Merch Shelf Integration:** Collaborate with platforms like Teespring to sell custom merchandise directly through your YouTube channel's merch shelf.

- **Promoting Merch in Videos:** Creatively promote your merchandise in your videos without being too intrusive, such as showcasing it subtly in the video or mentioning it briefly.

5. Sponsored Content and Brand Partnerships:

- **Securing Sponsorships:** Reach out to brands or use platforms like Famebit to secure sponsorships. Create content that incorporates the sponsored product or service.

- **Maintaining Authenticity:** Ensure that any sponsored content aligns with your channel's theme and values, maintaining authenticity to keep your audience's trust.

6. Digital Products and Courses:

- **Creating and Selling Digital Products:** Leverage your expertise to create and sell digital products like eBooks, courses, or guides.

- **Promotion Through Videos:** Use your videos to promote these digital products, providing insights or teasers about the content offered.

7. Patreon and Crowdfunding:

- **Setting Up Patreon:** Create a Patreon account for your channel, offering exclusive content, early access, or other perks to patrons.

- **Crowdfunding for Projects:** Utilize platforms like Kickstarter for specific projects related to your channel, inviting your audience to support.

8. Licensing Content:

- **Content Licensing:** If your content is unique or goes viral, you can license it to media outlets or other platforms for a fee.

- **Negotiating Deals:** Work with agencies or directly negotiate deals for the use of your content.

9. Utilizing Analytics for Monetization:

Optimizing Content for Revenue: Use insights from analytics to tweak your content strategy, focusing on what drives the most revenue.

Remember to create engaging and valuable content consistently, optimize your video titles, descriptions, and tags using relevant keywords, and actively promote your channel on social media and other online platforms to attract a wider audience. As your subscriber base and viewership grow, you will have more opportunities to collaborate with brands, negotiate higher rates, and earn a steady income from your faceless YouTube channel.

By implementing these techniques and monetization strategies, you can unlock the full potential of creating faceless YouTube channels, harnessing the power of AI tools to generate compelling content, engage with viewers, and build a successful online income stream.

Chapter Four

Virtual Influencers

Virtual influencers are a groundbreaking development in the digital world. They are created using sophisticated AI algorithms and advanced graphic design techniques. These influencers aren't real people; they are digital personas that can look and interact like human influencers. The technology behind them enables lifelike expressions, movements, and interactions, making them almost indistinguishable from real humans in the digital space.

Characteristics of Virtual Influencers:

The unique aspect of virtual influencers is their complete availability and adaptability. They can be tailored to fit any campaign, brand image, or marketing strategy. Unlike human influencers, they are not bound by physical limitations or personal schedules. This means they can be anywhere at any time, participating in global campaigns simultaneously without the logistical challenges of travel or scheduling.

Growth in the Market:

Virtual influencers are rapidly gaining popularity. A prime example is Lil Miquela, a virtual influencer with millions of followers on social media. She has collaborated with major brands, graced magazine covers, and even released music. This rising trend points to a significant shift in how brands approach marketing, with a growing acceptance and demand for virtual personas in advertising.

Control and Consistency:

One of the biggest advantages of virtual influencers is the degree of control brands have over their actions, messaging, and appearance. This control extends to ensuring consistent branding and messaging across all platforms and campaigns. They can be customized to align perfectly with brand values and aesthetics, something that's not always possible with human influencers.

Scalability and Flexibility:

Virtual influencers offer unparalleled scalability and flexibility. They can be part of multiple campaigns across different locations simultaneously. This eliminates the logistical and financial constraints often associated with organizing international photoshoots with human models.

Building Relationships with Audiences:

Despite being AI creations, virtual influencers can engage and build authentic relationships with their audience. Through consistent and well-crafted social media posts, they can develop a persona that resonates with followers. By interacting with followers, participating in trending challenges, and showing 'personal' sides, they create a sense of relatability.

Cross-Cultural and Demographic Appeal:

Virtual influencers can transcend cultural and demographic barriers. Their appearances and personalities can be crafted to appeal to diverse global audiences, something that's challenging with human influencers. This makes them incredibly valuable in global marketing strategies.

Ethical Considerations:

Transparency is crucial. Brands must disclose the AI nature of these influencers to maintain audience trust. Ethical concerns, such as promoting unrealistic beauty standards or impacting the human influencer market, must be addressed thoughtfully. It's important to strike a balance between innovation and ethical responsibility in their deployment.

Creating Virtual Influencers Using AI Tools

The creation of virtual influencers is a somewhat meticulous process that blends creativity with advanced technology. Using AI tools, you can develop a virtual influencer from concept to a fully-realized digital persona.

Design and Development:

- **Character Design:** Begin with conceptualizing your virtual influencer's appearance. Consider factors like age, style, personality traits, and cultural elements to appeal to your target audience. Tools like Midjourney are used for creating detailed, lifelike 3D models. Then you can refine and further build out the model using Stable Diffusion.

- **AI Integration:** Incorporate AI to bring your character to life. AI technologies, especially those focusing on natural language processing and generation, like OpenAI's GPT-4, can be trained to create realistic dialogues and interactions. AI can also be programmed to understand and respond to specific keywords or topics, making the influencer's interactions seem more natural and human-like.

Personality and Backstory:

- **Creating a Persona:** Develop a comprehensive backstory and personality for your virtual influencer. This includes their likes, dislikes, hobbies, and even opinions on current events. This backstory will guide their interactions, posts, and overall presence on social media.

- **Consistency in Character:** It's crucial to maintain consistency in the influencer's personality across all platforms.

This consistency helps in building a believable and engaging character that audiences can relate to.

Voice and Speech Synthesis:

- **Voice Creation:** Tools like Eleven Labs can be used to create a unique voice for your virtual influencer. The voice tone, pace, and accent should align with the influencer's personality and target audience.

- **Scriptwriting and Dialogue:** Utilize AI writing tools for scriptwriting. These scripts form the basis of the influencer's spoken content in videos or interactive platforms.

Integrating with Social Media Platforms:

- **Content Scheduling:** Utilize social media management tools like Hootsuite to schedule posts, videos, and interactions. This helps in maintaining a regular presence online.

- **Interaction with Followers:** Implement AI to manage basic interactions with followers. However, maintain a balance with human oversight to ensure appropriateness and authenticity.

Negotiating Brand Sponsorships and Creating an Influencer Agency

Once you have established your virtual influencer, the next step is to leverage their digital presence for brand sponsorships and potentially create an influencer agency. This phase is crucial for monetization and expanding the influencer's reach.

Negotiating Brand Sponsorships:

- **Identifying Potential Brands:** Look for brands whose products or services align with the virtual influencer's persona and audience. Use market research tools to identify brands that are actively seeking innovative marketing approaches.

- **Pitching to Brands:** Create a compelling pitch that highlights the unique benefits of partnering with a virtual influencer, such as controlled messaging, global reach, and the ability to create tailored content.

- **Portfolio and Metrics:** Present a portfolio of the virtual influencer's content, along with metrics on audience engagement, reach, and demographic data. This information can be crucial in convincing brands of the influencer's marketing potential.

- **Negotiation and Contracts:** When negotiating with brands, consider the scope of the campaign, deliverables, duration, and compensation. Ensure all agreements are formalized in contracts to avoid future disputes.

Creating an Influencer Agency:

- **Expanding Beyond a Single Influencer:** Once you have successfully established a virtual influencer, consider creating an agency that manages multiple virtual influencers. This allows for diversification and the ability to cater to various market segments.

- **Building a Team:** Assemble a team that specializes in different aspects of virtual influencer management, including AI specialists, content creators, marketers, and negotiation experts.

- **Services Offering:** Your agency can offer a range of services, including custom virtual influencer creation, content production, campaign management, and analytics reporting.

- **Networking and Promotion:** Network within the industry to build relationships with potential clients. Promote your agency through digital marketing, industry events, and collaborations.

Agency Operations and Management:

- **Client Management:** Develop a system for managing client relationships, from the initial contact and proposal to campaign execution and reporting.

- **Quality Control:** Ensure high standards of quality in the content and interactions of your virtual influencers. Regularly update their personas and capabilities to keep up with market trends.

- **Ethical Considerations:** Address ethical considerations proactively, including transparency about the AI nature of the influencers and adherence to advertising standards.

Scaling and Growth:

- **Scalability:** Consider how to scale your agency as demand grows. This might include creating new virtual influencers, expanding your team, or exploring new markets.

- **Staying Ahead of Trends:** Keep abreast of technological advancements and marketing trends to ensure your agency stays ahead of the curve and continues to offer innovative solutions.

Chapter Five

Email Copywriting

Offering Email Copywriting Services: Mastering the Art of Email Communication with AI Assistance

Understanding Email Copywriting:

- **What is Email Copywriting?** It's the process of writing compelling email content aimed at achieving specific marketing goals. This could be to drive sales, increase customer engagement, inform about a new product, or nurture customer relationships.

- **The Importance of Email Copywriting:** In a world where inboxes are flooded with messages, standing out with engaging and relevant content is key. Well-crafted emails can lead to higher open and click-through rates, building brand loyalty and driving conversions.

The Role of AI in Email Copywriting:

- **Automating and Enhancing Content Creation:** AI tools like ChatGPT, Jasper, or Copy.ai are designed to generate creative and effective email content quickly. These tools use machine learning to analyze successful email patterns and replicate their effectiveness in new content. You can even train it based on writing you like by uploading documents from your favorite Copywriters.

- **Personalization at Scale:** One of AI's most significant advantages is its ability to personalize content at scale. It can segment audiences and tailor messages according to individual preferences or past interactions, making each email feel more personal and relevant.

Crafting Professional and Promotional Emails Using AI:

- **Professional Emails:** AI can assist in creating professional emails that are clear, concise, and on-brand. These are often informational or communication-based emails sent to clients, stakeholders, or within an organization.

- **Promotional Emails:** For marketing and sales efforts, AI can help draft compelling promotional emails. These are designed to attract attention, showcase offers or products, and persuade the reader to take action, like making a purchase or signing up for an event.

Integrating AI with Human Insight:

- **Combining AI Efficiency with Human Creativity:** While AI provides a strong foundation and efficiency in creating email drafts, the human touch is vital for adding nuance, creativity, and ensuring brand alignment.

- **Quality Assurance:** It's crucial to review and refine AI-generated content to maintain a high standard. This ensures the final output resonates with the target audience and meets the specific objectives of the email campaign.

Expanding Your Skillset in Email Copywriting:

Building a Diverse Portfolio: Showcase a range of email copywriting skills, from transactional and informational to promotional and persuasive emails. This portfolio can demonstrate your versatility and effectiveness as an email copywriter.

Building a Client Base for Email Writing Services

Having mastered the art of crafting compelling emails with AI assistance, the next crucial step is to build a client base. This involves reaching out to potential clients who can benefit from your services and establishing yourself as a skilled email copywriter.

Identifying Your Target Market:

- **Define Your Niche:** Start by identifying the type of businesses that can benefit most from your services. This could be small startups, e-commerce platforms, B2B companies, or any other sector that relies heavily on email communication.

- **Understand Their Needs:** Research the common challenges and needs in your chosen niche. For instance, e-commerce sites might need engaging promotional emails, while B2B clients may require more informational or newsletter content.

Understanding the Market Value:

- **Industry Rates:** Email copywriting can vary widely in rates. On average, freelancers may charge anywhere from $50 to $300 per email, depending on the complexity, length, and the client's industry. For monthly newsletter services, rates might range from $500 to $2,000 per month.

- **Factors Affecting Rates:** Your pricing can be influenced by factors such as your experience, the client's budget, the industry standard, and the specific requirements of the campaign.

Projecting Potential Earnings:

- **Starting Out:** In the initial stages, earnings might be lower as you build your portfolio and client base. For example, you might start by earning $500 - $1,000 per month by managing a few smaller campaigns.

- **Growth Over Time:** As you gain more clients and your reputation grows, your potential earnings can significantly increase. An established email copywriter can earn between $3,000 to $30,000 per month, handling multiple clients or more extensive campaigns.

Marketing Your Services:

- **Create a Compelling Offering:** Develop a clear and attractive offering that outlines the benefits of your services. Emphasize the role of AI in enhancing the quality and effectiveness of your email campaigns.

- **Utilize Digital Marketing Channels:** Leverage platforms like LinkedIn, your professional website, or industry-specific forums to market your services. Engaging content that showcases your expertise in email copywriting can attract potential clients.

Networking and Building Relationships:

- **Attend Industry Events:** Participate in webinars, workshops, and conferences related to digital marketing and AI. Networking can lead to referrals and client leads.

- **Build Relationships Online:** Engage with potential clients on social media, answer questions on platforms like Quora, or write informative blog posts. These activities position you as a knowledgeable authority in the field.

Crafting a Winning Proposal:

- **Tailored Proposals:** When reaching out to potential clients, customize your proposals to address their specific needs and challenges. Highlight how your unique skills and AI-assisted approach can provide value to their business.

- **Showcase Results:** Include case studies or examples of successful email campaigns you've worked on. Real-world results can significantly bolster your proposal.

Setting Up Client Meetings:

- **Initial Consultations:** Offer free initial consultations to discuss potential clients' email marketing needs. This gives you an opportunity to further demonstrate your expertise and understanding of their business.

- **Listening and Understanding:** Use these meetings to understand their goals, target audience, and brand voice. This understanding is crucial for crafting emails that align with their overall marketing strategy.

Closing the Deal:

- **Clear Communication:** Be clear about your pricing, the scope of services, and the expected outcomes. Transparent communication helps in building trust.

- **Follow-up:** After the meeting, follow up with a summary of what was discussed and the next steps. Prompt follow-up demonstrates professionalism and your keenness to work with them.

Client Retention:

Chapter Six

Managing Twitter Accounts with AI

Managing Twitter Accounts with AI: Developing Engaging Content for Twitter

Twitter, offers unique opportunities for generating income, making it a valuable asset for businesses, influencers, and individuals. With its vast user base and real-time interaction capabilities, Twitter has become a hub for marketing, brand building, and audience engagement. In this context, efficiently managing a Twitter account using AI tools can not only enhance your online presence but also significantly contribute to your income generation strategies.

Understanding AI's Role in Twitter Management:

- **Content Generation:** AI tools like ChatGPT, Hootsuite's AI content assistant, or Buffer can help generate tweet ideas, create drafts, and even suggest optimal posting times based on audience engagement patterns.

- **Trend Analysis:** AI algorithms can analyze trending topics relevant to your niche, ensuring your content is timely and resonates with current events or popular discussions.

Crafting Engaging Tweets with AI:

- **Automated Tweet Creation:** Use AI to generate tweets that are engaging, witty, or informative. AI can help you maintain a consistent posting schedule with content that captures your brand's voice and message.

- **Personalization and Localization:** AI can tailor content based on your audience's demographics and interests, making tweets more relatable and targeted.

Enhancing Tweet Performance:

- **Hashtag and Keyword Optimization:** AI tools can suggest relevant hashtags and keywords to improve your tweets' visibility and reach.

- **A/B Testing:** Implement A/B testing on different tweet formats and contents to see what resonates best with your followers. AI can help analyze the results and adapt your content strategy accordingly.

Curating Content:

- **AI-Powered Content Curation:** Employ AI to curate content from various sources that align with your brand's ethos and audience's interests. This helps in maintaining a balanced and diverse content mix on your Twitter feed.

- **Content Scheduling:** Use AI tools to figure out your peak engagement times, ensuring your content reaches the maximum number of followers.

Interacting with Followers:

- **Automated Responses:** Set up AI-driven automated responses for common queries or comments. This can improve engagement and ensure timely interaction with your audience.

- **Sentiment Analysis:** Utilize AI for sentiment analysis to gauge the reaction of your audience to your content. This can inform future content and engagement strategies.

Analytics and Insights:

Monetizing Your Twitter Account: Exploring Diverse Revenue Streams

Twitter has evolved into a platform not just for social interaction but also for significant income generation. With the introduction of payment options by Twitter, the scope for monetization has expanded, offering multiple avenues for creators and businesses to earn revenue.

1. **Twitter Ad Revenue Sharing Program**:

   - **Program Overview**: Twitter's Creator Ads Revenue Sharing program allows users to profit from the ads displayed on their profiles, particularly those in tweet replies. This program is designed to support content creators by sharing Twitter's revenue directly with them, encouraging them to bring their audience to the platform.

   - **Eligibility and Payouts**: To qualify, accounts must have at least 5 million impressions on tweets over the previous three months, subscribe to Twitter Blue or be part of Verified Organizations, and pass a human review for creator monetization standards. Payouts for accounts with a few million followers have ranged from a few thousand dollars to almost $40,000.

   - **Revenue Sharing Details**: For earnings up to $50,000, Twitter lets content creators keep up to 92% of their earnings, which decreases to 80% after reaching that threshold. The program initially pays creators the entire amount Twitter receives, minus payment gateway fees, with 70% for subscriptions on iOS & Android and about 92% on the web.

- **Examples of Earnings**: Conservative YouTuber Benny Johnson reported qualifying for close to $10,000, while the @Elon_alerts account, which tweets about Elon Musk, stated their compensation was roughly $2,200.

2. **Other Monetization Strategies**:

- **Sponsored Tweets**: Partner with brands to promote their products or services in your tweets. You can negotiate a flat fee or a commission on sales.

- **Affiliate Marketing**: Promote products or services on Twitter and earn a commission for each sale you generate through your affiliate links.

- **Subscriptions**: Charge followers a monthly fee to access exclusive content or features on your Twitter account.

- **Tips**: Enable a feature where followers can send you money directly through Twitter.

3. **Building and Monetizing Your Twitter Account**:

- **Grow Your Following**: Consistently tweet engaging and relevant content to attract and retain followers. Engagement with your audience is key.

- **Create High-Quality Content**: Ensure your tweets are informative, visually appealing, and authentic to build trust and credibility with your audience.

- **Strategic Content Planning**: Use analytics to understand what content resonates with your audience and plan your tweets accordingly to maximize engagement and monetization opportunities.

By effectively utilizing AI in managing your Twitter account, you can save time, increase engagement, and grow your online presence. However, it is essential to strike a balance between automation and authentic human interaction. AI should enhance your Twitter management strategy, not replace it entirely. With the right approach, AI can be a powerful ally in successfully managing your Twitter account and achieving your social media goals.

Chapter Seven

TikToks & Youtube Shorts

Creating TikTok's and YouTube Shorts for businesses and influencers is a highly relevant and profitable skill in today's digital landscape. Here's an in-depth look at why this skill is valuable:

Expanding Reach and Engagement: TikTok and YouTube Shorts have emerged as leading platforms for short-form video content. Their algorithm-driven nature means content has a higher chance of reaching a wide audience, including those outside a brand's existing followers. This reach is vital for businesses and influencers looking to expand their digital footprint.

Adaptability to Current Trends: Short videos are perfect for tapping into current trends, memes, or challenges, making them a dynamic tool for staying relevant and engaging with the audience.

Effective Storytelling in Bite-Sized Content: Short-form videos require concise, impactful storytelling, which can be more effective than

Effortless TikTok and YouTube Shorts

Creating engaging TikTok and YouTube Shorts for businesses and influencers involves leveraging tools like OpusClip. Here's how to go about it:

1. **Source Video Selection**: Identify compelling source videos that align with the brand's messaging or influencer's persona. These could be existing content pieces or specially created footage.

2. **Using OpusClip**: OpusClip streamlines the editing process. Simply paste the link of the source video into the tool. It automatically clips segments, saving significant editing time.

3. **Editing and Refinement**: Although OpusClip often gets it right, occasionally you may need to make slight edits for better alignment with your messaging or branding.

4. **Direct Use**: Many times, the clips created by OpusClip are ready to use, requiring minimal to no adjustments, making the process efficient and straightforward.

This method allows for quick, effective creation of short-form content, tapping into the power of TikTok and YouTube Shorts with minimal technical hassle.

Marketing Your Video Creation Services to Businesses and Influencers

To successfully market your service of creating TikTok and YouTube Shorts for businesses and influencers, follow these steps:

1. **Identify Your Target Audience**: Focus on businesses and influencers who actively use or want to start using TikTok

and YouTube Shorts. Look for those who lack the time or skills to create engaging short-form content themselves.

2. **Develop a Portfolio**: Create a collection of sample videos showcasing your skills. Use various styles and themes to demonstrate versatility.

3. **Leverage Social Media and Networking**: Utilize platforms like LinkedIn, Instagram, and Twitter to connect with potential clients. Share your work, engage in relevant conversations, and build professional relationships.

4. **Offer Tailored Solutions**: Understand the specific needs of each client and offer customized services. For businesses, focus on brand promotion and customer engagement. For influencers, emphasize creativity and trends to boost their online presence.

5. **Use Testimonials and Case Studies**: Showcase successful projects and client testimonials to build credibility. Case studies can illustrate the impact of your work on a client's social media engagement and reach.

6. **Create Attractive Service Packages**: Offer different packages based on client needs, from basic editing to full content creation and strategy planning.

7. **Advertise Your Services**: Consider paid advertising on social media or Google Ads targeting specific industry niches.

8. **Collaborate and Network**: Attend industry events and webinars to network with potential clients. Collaborations with other creators or agencies can also expand your reach.

9. **Email Marketing**: Send targeted emails to potential clients
   with an introduction to your services and examples of your
   work.

By following these steps, you can effectively market your video
creation services, attracting both businesses and influencers looking to
enhance their presence on TikTok and YouTube Shorts.

Chapter Eight

Book Summaries

Writing and Monetizing AI-Generated Book Summaries: Selecting Books and Creating Summaries

Creating and monetizing AI-generated book summaries can be a lucrative endeavor, especially for audiences seeking quick insights into various books. Here's how to get started:

1. **Choosing the Right Books**: Focus on popular or trending books, bestsellers, and highly-rated titles. Consider genres and topics that resonate with your target audience, such as self-help, business, technology, or fiction.

2. **Using AI for Summarization**: Leverage AI tools to generate concise and accurate summaries. Tools like OpenAI's GPT-3 can process the text and produce coherent, condensed versions that capture the essential points and themes.

3. **Adding Personal Touch**: While AI provides a base, personalize the summaries by adding unique insights, critiques, or

contextual information to enhance value.

4. **Ensuring Quality**: Review and refine AI-generated content to ensure accuracy and readability, maintaining the original book's tone and intent.

By following these steps, you can create valuable book summaries that appeal to readers seeking knowledge without the commitment of reading entire books. This service is particularly appealing to busy professionals, students, and avid readers looking to expand their knowledge efficiently.

Incorporating Affiliate Marketing with AI-Generated Book Summaries

Combining AI-generated book summaries with affiliate marketing can significantly enhance your monetization strategy. Here's how to do it:

1. **Affiliate Partnerships with Book Retailers**: Establish affiliations with book retailers like Amazon, Barnes & Noble and include Audible, an audiobook service. Affiliate links to both physical books and their audiobook versions can be embedded in your summaries.

2. **Targeted Summaries for Affiliate Books**: Focus your AI-generated summaries on books available through your affiliate partners. This alignment ensures that every summary has the potential to generate affiliate income.

3. **CTAs within Summaries**: Incorporate clear and compelling calls-to-action in your summaries, encouraging read-

ers to purchase the book using your affiliate link.

4. **Balancing Value and Promotion**: While the goal is to promote book sales through affiliate links, ensure your summaries provide genuine value to the reader. This balance is crucial for maintaining credibility and audience trust.

5. **Leveraging Social Media and Blogs**: Share your summaries on social media platforms and blogs, embedding affiliate links within these posts to reach a wider audience.

6. **SEO Optimization**: Optimize your content for search engines to increase visibility. Use relevant keywords related to the books and summaries to attract organic traffic.

By strategically incorporating affiliate marketing into your AI-generated book summaries, you can create a sustainable income stream while providing valuable content to your audience.

Platforms for Publishing and Promoting AI-Generated Book Summaries

To effectively publish and promote your AI-generated book summaries, consider using a mix of online platforms that cater to diverse audiences:

1. **Personal Blog or Website**: Create a dedicated website or blog where you can regularly post your book summaries. This centralizes your content and establishes your brand. This also allows you to create your own Funnel and control your landing page.

2. **Social Media Platforms**: Utilize platforms like Twitter,

LinkedIn, and Facebook to share your summaries and engage with your audience. These platforms are excellent for building a community and driving traffic to your website.

3. **Medium**: Publish your summaries on Medium, a popular blogging platform, to reach a broader audience interested in literature and learning.

4. **Goodreads**: Share shorter versions of your summaries on Goodreads, a community for book lovers, with links back to your full summaries.

5. **Email Newsletters**: Build an email list and send out regular newsletters with your latest summaries, updates, and affiliate links.

6. **Amazon Kindle Direct Publishing (KDP)**: Consider compiling your summaries into an eBook and publishing it on Amazon KDP.

7. **YouTube**: Create and share video summaries, which can be particularly engaging and attract a different audience segment.

By leveraging these platforms, you can effectively publish and promote your AI book summaries, attracting a wide range of readers and maximizing the reach of your affiliate marketing efforts.

Chapter Nine

Resume Writing Services Using AI

Offering resume writing services using AI is a highly lucrative and in-demand skill in today's job market. Here's why this service is a great income generator:

1. **High Demand**: In a competitive job market, job seekers are constantly looking for ways to stand out. Professional resume services are in high demand, especially among recent graduates, career changers, and those looking to climb the career ladder.

2. **Efficiency and Scale**: AI streamlines the resume writing process, allowing you to handle a higher volume of clients without compromising on quality.

3. **Customization and Optimization**: AI's ability to customize and optimize resumes for specific job postings makes your service more attractive, as it increases the client's

chances of getting noticed by recruiters.

4. **Diverse Clientele**: You can cater to a wide range of clients from different industries and career levels, expanding your market reach.

5. **Remote Work Opportunity**: This service can be offered remotely, appealing to freelancers or entrepreneurs seeking flexible, location-independent work.

By tapping into this service area, you can leverage AI to offer efficient, tailored, and high-quality resume writing services, meeting the needs of a broad client base and generating significant income.

Finding Clients and Building a Resume Writing Service

Building a successful resume writing service involves strategic client acquisition and business growth. Here's how to find clients and establish your service:

1. **Online Presence**: Create a professional website showcasing your services, portfolio, and client testimonials. Utilize SEO to enhance visibility.

2. **Networking**: Leverage LinkedIn and other professional networks to connect with potential clients. Attend career fairs and workshops.

3. **Partnerships**: Collaborate with career coaches, recruitment agencies, and educational institutions to receive referrals.

4. **Social Media Marketing**: Use platforms like LinkedIn,

Facebook, and Instagram for advertising and sharing valuable content related to career development.

5. **Freelancing Platforms**: Register on sites like Upwork, Fiverr, and Freelancer to reach clients looking for resume writing services.

6. **Content Marketing**: Publish blogs and articles on resume writing tips and job market trends to attract clients and establish authority in the field.

7. **Referral Programs**: Encourage existing clients to refer others by offering discounts or additional services.

8. **Client Reviews and Testimonials**: Showcase successful case studies and client testimonials to build credibility.

9. **Customized Packages**: Offer various packages catering to different needs, such as entry-level, executive, or industry-specific resumes.

By mastering the techniques for creating professional resumes using AI, implementing effective strategies for finding clients, and staying up-to-date with industry trends, you can build a successful resume writing service that sets you apart in the competitive job market. Embrace the power of AI to streamline your resume writing process and help job seekers achieve their career goals. With a strong online presence, collaboration with industry professionals, and a portfolio of successful resumes, you can establish yourself as a trusted and sought-after resume writer in the AI era.

Chapter Ten

E-Commerce Product Descriptions with AI

Writing AI-generated product descriptions for e-commerce stores is a highly profitable and in-demand skill. This service is essential for online retailers who want to make their products stand out in the crowded online space. Here's why this venture is lucrative:

1. **Growing E-Commerce Market**: With the rapid expansion of online shopping, there's a constant need for fresh, SEO-optimized, and engaging product descriptions.

2. **Value to Online Retailers**: Effective product descriptions directly influence purchase decisions, making them a valuable asset for online stores.

3. **Efficiency with AI**: AI can produce high-quality descriptions quickly, allowing you to serve more clients and handle large volumes of work.

4. **SEO and Conversion Optimization**: Skillfully written descriptions using AI can significantly improve a product's search engine ranking and conversion rates.

5. **Customization for Diverse Products**: AI's adaptability allows you to cater to a wide range of products and industries, broadening your potential client base.

6. **Remote and Scalable Business Model**: This service can be provided remotely, offering flexibility, and it's easily scalable as your client base grows.

By offering AI-assisted e-commerce product description services, you can tap into the lucrative online retail market, providing a service that enhances both the visibility and sales potential of products.

Integrating SEO and Marketing Strategies in AI-Generated E-Commerce Product Descriptions

Effective e-commerce product descriptions should integrate both SEO and marketing strategies to maximize their impact. Here's how you can do it:

1. **Keyword Optimization**: Use AI tools for keyword research to identify high-ranking keywords relevant to each product. Incorporate these keywords naturally into the descriptions.

2. **Compelling Meta Descriptions**: Create engaging meta descriptions with AI assistance, capturing the essence of the

product while using targeted keywords for better search engine visibility.

3. **Emphasize Unique Selling Points (USPs)**: AI can help identify and highlight the USPs of products, making them stand out in the market.

4. **Customer-Centric Language**: Use AI to tailor the language of your product descriptions to resonate with your target audience, enhancing relatability and appeal.

5. **Cross-Promotion Tactics**: Integrate AI to suggest related products, encouraging cross-selling and increasing average order value.

6. **Analytics-Driven Updates**: Utilize AI to analyze customer feedback and performance metrics, refining product descriptions for better performance.

By combining SEO and marketing strategies in your AI-generated product descriptions, you can significantly boost the online presence and sales potential of e-commerce products.

Chapter Eleven

Creating and Selling Digital Products

In today's digital age, creating and selling digital products like eBooks, guides, and courses is an increasingly lucrative venture. Here's why this approach is a profitable income stream:

1. **Vast Market Demand**: The digital landscape is rapidly expanding, with a growing demand for diverse and easily accessible learning materials, guides, and courses. This surge in digital consumption opens up numerous opportunities for creators to cater to varied interests and niches.

2. **Low Overhead and High Profitability**: Digital products eliminate the need for physical materials, production, and shipping, drastically reducing overhead costs. This leads to significantly higher profit margins compared to traditional

physical products.

3. **Global Reach and Accessibility**: The internet erases geographical boundaries, allowing creators to reach and sell to a global audience. This expands the potential customer base far beyond local markets.

4. **Passive Income Stream**: Once created, digital products can be sold repeatedly with little to no additional cost, providing a sustainable source of passive income. This is particularly appealing for those looking to generate revenue without the constant need for new output.

5. **Flexibility and Scalability**: Digital products offer the flexibility to start small and scale up. Creators can begin with simpler, less time-intensive products and gradually move to more complex offerings as they gain experience and audience insights.

6. **Customization and Personalization**: Digital products can be easily updated or customized to meet evolving market trends or specific customer needs, ensuring long-term relevance and appeal.

7. **Creative Freedom and Personal Branding**: This venture allows creators to express their unique perspectives and expertise, building a personal brand that resonates with their audience.

Overall, creating and selling digital products is not just financially rewarding but also creatively fulfilling, offering a platform for individuals to share their knowledge, skills, and passions with a global audience.

Choosing a profitable topic for creating a digital product involves a strategic approach to ensure market demand and interest. Here's a step-by-step process:

In-Depth Market Research for Profitable Niches

1. **Using Google Trends and SEMrush**: For example, if you're interested in creating a digital guide on home gardening, you would first go to Google Trends. Here, you can type in "home gardening" and analyze the interest over time and by regions. This will give you an idea of the demand for the topic.

2. Next, head to SEMrush. In SEMrush, input the same keyword and look at the 'Keyword Overview' section. You'll get details on search volume (how many people are searching for this term monthly) and keyword difficulty (a score showing how hard it would be to rank for this keyword in Google).

3. **Identifying Customer Pain Points**: Read forums like Reddit or Quora, focusing on gardening sections. Look for frequently asked questions or problems people are facing. For instance, you might find that a lot of beginners struggle with pest control. This insight can guide the focus of your digital product.

Creating an eBook or Course with AI and Tools:

1. **Topic Selection and Research**: Use AI tools like OpenAI's ChatGPT for brainstorming and refining your eBook or course topic. Tap into AI's vast database to research current trends, gather information, and identify gaps in existing materials.

2. **Outline Creation**: Leverage AI to help structure your content. It can assist in developing a coherent outline, organizing chapters for an eBook or modules for a course, ensuring logical progression and comprehensive coverage of the topic.

3. **Content Development**: Utilize AI writing assistants for drafting content. They can generate initial drafts, suggest ideas, or even write entire sections, significantly speeding up the creation process. Remember to add your unique insights and expertise to personalize the content.

4. **Design and Visuals**: For eBooks, use design platforms like Canva or Adobe InDesign for a professional layout and appealing cover design. For online courses, tools such as Teachable or Thinkific provide user-friendly interfaces to organize and present your course material engagingly.

5. **Interactive Elements**: Incorporate interactive elements like quizzes or exercises using tools like Typeform or Quizlet, especially for courses, to enhance user engagement and retention of the material.

6. **Editing and Proofreading**: Use editing tools like Grammarly or Hemingway Editor for refining language, grammar, and overall readability. This step ensures your content is polished and professional.

7. **Publication and Hosting**: For eBooks, explore self-publishing platforms such as Amazon Kindle Direct Publishing. For online courses, consider hosting them on platforms like Udemy or Coursera, which also offer the benefit of a built-in audience.

8. **Testing and Feedback**: Before the final launch, test your eBook or course with a small audience group. Gather feedback and make necessary adjustments. This iterative process ensures that your final product resonates well with your target audience.

Effective Marketing Strategies

1. **Instagram Marketing**: If your digital product is visually appealing, like a gardening guide with lots of images, Instagram can be a powerful tool. Share tips from your guide, create short how-to videos, and use gardening-related hashtags to attract an audience.

2. **Email Marketing Campaigns**: Build an email list by offering a free mini-guide on a popular topic, like "Top 5 Organic Fertilizers." Once people sign up, send a series of emails that provide value and gently introduce your comprehensive gardening guide.

3. **Running Paid Ads**: Leverage paid advertising on platforms like Facebook, Instagram, and Google AdWords. For your gardening guide, target ads to gardening enthusiasts, peo-

ple interested in sustainable living, or those who frequently purchase gardening supplies online. Use eye-catching visuals from your guide and compelling ad copy that highlights the unique value of your product. Set a budget and closely monitor the performance of your ads, adjusting targeting and content based on the response and engagement you receive. Paid ads can help you reach a broader audience and drive more direct sales of your digital product.

Pricing and Monetization

1. **Analyze Competitors' Pricing**: Look at similar gardening eBooks on Amazon. Note their prices and reader reviews to understand what readers appreciate and what they feel is lacking.

2. **Affiliate Integration**: In your eBook, you can include links to recommended gardening tools or products available on Amazon. Join the Amazon Associates program to earn commissions from these links.

Choosing the Right Platforms

1. **Amazon Kindle for eBooks**: Use Amazon's Kindle Direct Publishing for your eBook. Optimize your product listing with a catchy title, a compelling book description incorporating keywords, and an attractive cover.

2. **Udemy for Courses**: If creating a video course, Udemy

is user-friendly. Ensure your course has a clear structure, with each section focusing on different aspects of gardening. Create a compelling course description using keywords like "beginner-friendly," "home gardening," etc.

Long-Term Growth Strategies

1. **Stay Updated with Trends**: Regularly update your digital product with new gardening techniques or trends. This keeps your content relevant and valuable.

2. **Expand to Related Topics**: After success with your first product, consider creating related guides, like "Advanced Home Gardening Techniques" or "Urban Gardening Secrets."

Throughout these steps, maintain a balance between AI-generated content and personal touch. Your unique insights, experiences, and teaching style will differentiate your digital product in a crowded market.

Chapter Twelve

AI Prompt Writing

In a world increasingly driven by AI, the ability to craft effective AI prompts is a crucial skill. As AI technologies like ChatGPT become more integral in various industries, the demand for skilled prompt writers is surging. Businesses, content creators, and tech enthusiasts alike are seeking individuals who can efficiently harness the power of AI to generate desired outcomes, whether for content creation, data analysis, or problem-solving.

Mastering AI prompt writing opens doors to numerous opportunities. It allows for precision in commanding AI tools, leading to more relevant, creative, and accurate outputs. This skill is not just about understanding AI but also about leveraging it to its fullest potential, making it a highly valuable and marketable asset in today's tech-driven landscape.

Crafting Effective AI Prompts: The Art of Commanding AI

1. **Understanding AI Capabilities**: Recognize the strengths and limitations of AI. Familiarize yourself with how AI interprets and responds to language nuances, context, and specific instructions.

2. **Clarity and Precision**: Ensure your prompts are clear and precise. Ambiguous or vague prompts can lead to irrelevant or unexpected responses from AI.

3. **Context Matters**: Provide sufficient context for complex requests. Context helps AI understand the background and the specific requirements of the task.

4. **Iterative Process**: Developing effective prompts is often an iterative process. Experiment with different phrasings and structures to see which yields the best results.

5. **Creative Use of Keywords**: Incorporate relevant keywords strategically. This guides the AI to stay on topic and cover specific aspects in its response.

6. **Setting the Tone and Style**: Indicate the desired tone and style, whether it's formal, casual, technical, or creative. This helps AI tailor its language and approach accordingly.

7. **Feedback Loop**: Use the AI's responses to refine your prompts. This feedback loop is crucial in honing the art of prompt writing.

8. **Continuous Learning**: Stay updated with advancements in AI capabilities and adapt your prompt crafting skills accordingly.

Mastering AI prompt writing is a valuable skill, enabling more effective and efficient use of AI tools for various applications.

Monetizing AI Prompt Writing Skills

Monetizing AI prompt writing skills involves identifying and capitalizing on opportunities where these skills are in high demand. Here are some effective ways to turn your expertise in AI prompt writing into a profitable venture:

1. **Freelance Services**: Offer your prompt writing skills on freelance platforms like Upwork, Fiverr, or Freelancer. Many businesses and individuals look for experts who can help them optimize their use of AI tools.

2. **Consulting**: Position yourself as an AI prompt writing consultant. Provide services to companies needing guidance on leveraging AI for content creation, data analysis, or customer service enhancements.

3. **Training and Workshops**: Conduct online workshops or create courses teaching others how to write effective AI prompts. Platforms like Udemy or Teachable are great for hosting such educational content.

4. **Content Creation**: Use your skills to create high-quality AI-generated content for blogs, websites, or social media, offering this as a service to content creators and digital marketers.

5. **Partnerships with AI Firms**: Collaborate with AI software companies, offering your expertise in refining their AI

prompt interfaces or training their clients in effective prompt usage.

6. **E-Book or Guide Creation**: Write and sell e-books or guides on AI prompt writing techniques, targeting audiences eager to learn about AI utilization.

By exploring these avenues, you can effectively monetize your AI prompt writing skills, tapping into a niche yet growing market.

Chapter Thirteen

Conclusion

In this book, we've explored the transformative potential of AI in creating diverse online income streams. From virtual influencers to AI-assisted content creation, the key takeaways highlight the vast opportunities AI offers for entrepreneurs, freelancers, and digital marketers. As you embark on this journey, remember:

1. **Embrace Continuous Learning**: AI and digital markets evolve rapidly. Stay informed and adaptable.

2. **Experiment and Innovate**: Don't hesitate to try new approaches or tools.

3. **Ethical Considerations**: Always prioritize transparency and ethical practices.

4. **Build a Strong Online Presence**: Whatever your niche, a solid online presence is crucial for success.

5. **Network and Collaborate**: Connect with peers and mentors for growth and opportunities.

Now that you've gained insights into the world of AI-driven income opportunities, it's time to take action. Choose a path that resonates with you, whether it's creating captivating digital content, managing AI-driven social media accounts, or crafting engaging AI-generated book summaries. Start small, experiment, and learn as you grow. The digital landscape is ripe with possibilities, and your unique contribution awaits. Remember, success in this field comes from taking that first step and persistently pursuing your goals. So, take that leap, embrace the power of AI, and start building your path to success today!

Your Voice is Valuable

I hope you've found value in these pages, I'd like to invite you to share your thoughts with a review. Your feedback helps me improve and helps the book reach more readers who can benefit from this knowledge.